Who am I?
A little book about finding yourself... with magic ingredients

First Published in Great Britain in 2019 by Balance Books Publishing

Kemp House, 142 - 160 City Road
London. EC1V 2NX

Enquiries to **editor@balancebookspublishing.com**

Copyright ©2019 Liz Bell.
The moral rights of the author have been asserted.

All rights reserved. No part of this publication may be reproduced, distributed, or transmitted in any form or by any means, including photocopying, recording, or other electronic or mechanical methods, without the prior written permission of the publisher, except in the case of brief quotations embodied in critical reviews and certain other non-commercial uses permitted by copyright law. For permission requests, write to the publisher, addressed "Attention: Permissions Coordinator," at the email address above.

Illustrator - Katie Watts
Cover and book design - Matt Underwood
Editor - Thea Hutchings

Printed and bound to FSC standards.

ISBN: 978-1-9993204-0-9

British Library Cataloguing in Publication Data. A catalogue record for this book is available from the British Library

Who am I?

**A little book about finding yourself...
with magic ingredients**

Written by Liz Bell
Illustrations by Katie Watts

Acknowledgements and Gratitude

I am big on gratitude so it's important for me to thank and be grateful to a few people for our little book.

JoJo my partner in everything including this book. You are my constant and true love.

I wouldn't be who I am without my mum, dad and sister who have helped shape me into the person I have become and whom I love dearly. I truly hope mum can read this in heaven.

To all my family for putting up with me going on and on about the book for the last few years and for always being there when I need you, I love you all so much.

To Katie Watts our amazing illustrator; you outdid yourself and your kindness, hard work and dedication were a godsend. Can't wait to work together again.

Thea Hutchings my editor, grammar queen and EqUa's rock; you are amazing.

Lee Marriott my friend and confidante always.

To Kate Rawling my friend and on occasion writing partner, thanks for always being interested in anything I do; it always keeps me motivated.

To the Bloody Brilliant author Cathy Newman for bigging us up whenever she gets the chance - thank you, we are incredibly grateful.

To all my beautiful friends (you know who you are) who have supported me in all my endeavours, without you lot I'd be nothing.

My inspiring teachers most notably:

Ali Campbell (you started our journey and we will never be the same, thank you), Michael Neill, Mike Mandell and Chris Thompson, Richard Wiseman, Syd Banks, Milton H Erickson, Ruby Wax for her brilliant work in mindfulness, Gore and Lisa from The Body IQ Studio (our workshop and studio comrades) and with great reverence his Holiness The Dalai Lama for kindly letting us use his quote at the end of this book.

Last but not least, anyone who buys this book and dares to be all they can be. You are everything.

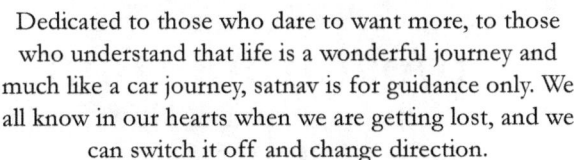

Dedicated to those who dare to want more, to those who understand that life is a wonderful journey and much like a car journey, satnav is for guidance only. We all know in our hearts when we are getting lost, and we can switch it off and change direction.

> " I am a coach of communication **most importantly** how we communicate, with **ourselves.** "
>
> Liz

Who I am

Liz Bell, Media Performance and Life Coach

In 2010 while listening to an all too familiar story from a colleague, Liz realised more and more of the people around her were consistently burnt out and stressed. This led to a swerve away from her then career path and started a 5-year quest in retraining.

First, she studied Psychology, and became something of an expert in body language. In 2012, she achieved Licenced NLP Practitioner status, certified by Dr Richard Bandler and finally, went on to gain additional qualifications in hypnotherapy and transformative life coaching.

She is proud to be one of a handful mentored by the world-renowned life coach Ali Campbell whose transformative life coaching style she says has been a revelation to learn.

Retraining meant Liz could help her past colleagues deal with the fast and often merciless media industry, but she soon realised that the skills and coaching style she practised could be put to an even wider audience.

She has since co-developed a unique approach to coaching called The EqUa Approach® which helps clients find their balance, equanimity and be truer to themselves.

Liz has a clientele of media and performance professionals, as well as those from all walks of life with phobias, anxiety, sleep problems, motivation loss and those who need help with weight management. But most importantly now you.

Contents

1 Introduction - How to use this book

2 Why am I? My purpose

3 Where am I? Am I in the moment?

4 What am I? Where do I fit?

5 When am I? Do I live in the past or the future?

6 Who am I? Letting go and being free!

Introduction

How to use this book

First, just breathe for a few moments. Just concentrate on your breath and breathe out any distractions.

Why not take this book in, let it be the only thing on your mind at this moment?

Be present.

Now I want you close your eyes and imagine you are somewhere beautiful to you, for as long as you want to and continue to breathe while you feel yourself there - wherever there may be.

Now you should be in a better changing state less distracted and more focused on whatever needs to happen.

This is going to be a totally new experience of self-help because I don't want you to do anything at all except read the book. No homework or tasks or bullet points or lists. Just read the stories then let them marinate.

I want you to open yourself up to another way of learning, another way of changing.

Ultimately, I want you to let go of anything you think you know about yourself and go on this little journey with me.

It doesn't have to mean anything, it doesn't have to mean everything, it doesn't even have to change
anything yet. Except for your willingness to begin - which is the most important thing of all.

Let go and begin.

My coaching partner Jo loves to use a rucksack of rocks as her example of all the things we carry with us, the rocks representing the baggage we choose to carry.

So I want you to imagine you have your own rucksack full of the things you carry with you and as we begin this journey, I want you to notice how heavy it is right now.

BUT

As you make your commitment to change you will notice it lighten just a little. Now I'm not saying it will be empty yet but it will certainly have a little less in it having committed to change.

So, as you begin the next chapter of your journey you can be proud of yourself because you will have lost some of the rocks of fear and doubt.

When you have read this book through try listening to it. Go to www.equacoaching.com/whoamiaudio for the audio version or get someone else to read it to you because this is where most of the magic happens. Follow the same instructions in the stories and take yourself through your own version of them.

Remember, don't rush it, do one at a time and let it sink in. It's better to let each one breathe on its own.

Let yourself enjoy them and you will really reap the benefits. Don't analyse or expect, just let it do its thing and soon enough you will understand how to be free to be you.

With love

Liz

> **Knowing yourself is the beginning of all wisdom.**
> — Aristotle

Chapter One

Why am I?

What's my purpose?

In a not so distant land, there was a not so distant house

and in that not so distant house there lived an ordinary family.

How do I know they were ordinary?

Because they said so.

Why does that make it so?

I guess they just know.

One day, the ordinary father decides to take the day off work from his ordinary job and spend the day with his ordinary children who are on their school holidays.

"Why am I so ordinary?"

he asks himself.

"I feel so lost, I want to be extraordinary so I'm going to go home and make it an unforgettably exciting day for my children and me.

Then they'll really see me, and how different I can be."

He asks the three of them

"What do you want to do today?"

They say

"We don't know but can it be exciting, different and extraordinary?"

The ordinary father rubs his chin and says
"Hmmmm. What does that mean to you?"

The first one takes a deep breath and cautiously says to him

"It means being busy all the time never standing still, looking and finding new things to learn."

The second one says

"To me, it means drifting off into a fantasy world where stories are reality and reality is a story."

The third one says

"It's about where we can feel noticed and be seen, to stand and shout and laugh and be heard."

"Wow," says their father

"I am at a loss. What could we possibly do to make you all three of you happy?"

He mulled over this quest for quite some time. He spoke to his friends and talked with his wife, he searched on the internet for hours but still couldn't find the perfect thing to do with his kids that day.

He hoped they realised how hard he was working to make it perfect, so they could all be happy.

All day long he looked for ideas but just couldn't find anything exciting enough that would fit all of their requests.

Eventually, the day passed by and the father had barely spent any time with his children, so dedicated was he to finding the most perfectly extraordinary day.

But alas finally he had to concede that he couldn't do it and eventually after resigning himself to defeat he said.

"I'm so sorry, I just couldn't come up with the right thing for us all to do."

His children looked at him confused and disappointed

They all said

"But we could have just gone for a walk, daddy"

"What?"

asked the dad crossly.

"But that's so ordinary and I wanted it to be perfect and different today and how would that have fitted all your requests?"

I'M sorry

ENCHANTED forest.

The first one said

"On a walk I would have been busy walking and seeing things, talking with you and learning about everything different that I saw."

The second one said

"If we went on a walk I could have made up a story about the people we met and we could have had gone into the enchanted forest up the road and I could have shown you all the fun things I see through my eyes."

The third one said

"If we had gone for a walk you would have been with us and talked to us. You would have seen us and heard us and noticed us."

Their father's faced dropped as he finally realised what he had been missing - not just today but for years, he had been so foolish and blind to miss all the extraordinary things in his life.

He smiled, then laughed and his children looked up at him even more confused.

"Are you OK daddy?"

He crouched down and hugged his children for a very long time and vowed to himself to never see ordinary in anything ever again.

Chapter Two

Where am I?

Am I in the moment?

Ollie wakes up in the morning and thinks

"I can't wait for my breakfast"

He has his breakfast, it's ok.

Then he thinks

"I can't wait to go outside"

He goes outside, it's ok.

At midday, he thinks

"I can't wait for my lunch"

He has lunch, it's ok

He then thinks

"I can't wait to go home"

He goes home, it's ok.

Now he's home he thinks

"I can't wait for my dinner"

He has his dinner, it's ok.

He can't wait for bed so tomorrow can start

At bedtime his mum says

"How was your day?"

Ollie says

"Dunno, I can't remember"

Chapter Three

What am I?

Where do I fit

I feel lost, I feel nothing...

But...

If I don't feel alive then what am I?

If I'm not awake then am I asleep?

If I am not good then am I bad?

If I'm not happy then am I sad?

What am I?

I am told by someone who seems happier than me to take a moment to see what is on the inside of me.

What IS it that makes me feel free?

Feel alive

Feel like me

How do I do that then, how do I see inside?

What if I don't like what I am inside?

Maybe I'm better off not going there

Not knowing

But I know that's not true.

Deep down inside

So what can I do to be brave enough to go there?

Then I see a circle in front of me, it's a beautiful colour that feels like mine and it is warm and friendly.

Immediately I feel like I want to step inside, it's asking me to.

So I do.

I close my eyes and take it in. This is a safe place, a comfortable place.

I've been here before and I can see myself laughing, confident and alive, it's my place, it's me.

What a lovely feeling this is, I like this so much I think of all the times I've felt like this before

the smells

the sounds

the pictures

I really feel all those things again.

It feels good and safe and brave and full of possibility.
I breathe it in as much as I can, till I'm full to the brim.

I step back outside the circle and I open my eyes on the outside.

It feels different like everything has a different shade
I am seeing things another way and everything feels calm and possible.

But what if I lose it, it's too good for me, surely I can't feel this good all the time but somehow I surprise myself because I know I can.

I feel braver now and somehow I know I can step back into my circle anytime I need to.

So I fold my circle it up and put it in my pocket safe for when that time comes.

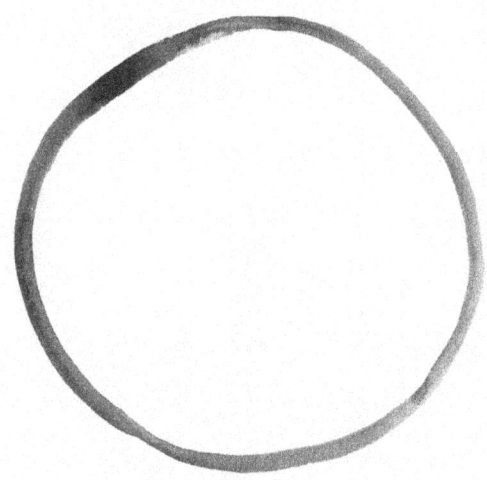

Chapter Four

When am I?

Do I live in the past or future?

Tick tock...

Time, time, time what is it that drives us so?

In time we find safety, in time we find a friend, a comfort, some solace.

But we lose ourselves in time too, it can berate us, taunt us, make us feel lost.

Which do you do, I wonder?

Let's go on a journey in time to see.

I want you to close your eyes and breathe, just think about time for a moment. Where does it feel to you?
Up, down, sideways, diagonally?

Where is your future?

Notice the direction

Where is your past?

Notice again

And of course, your present, where are you now?

Present is the only real time... tick tock... and here you are!

Now imagine you can float above yourself and look down on yourself.

Can you see yourself down below?

Which way do you want to go? Back, forward, stay put?

Let's go back.

Float along your line of time and see all the things that have shaped you. You might stop and linger over a few.

Take your time, after all, it is yours.

You may reflect

Take them all in, whichever you want to

Feel them

Hear them

Smell them and taste them, sometimes.

Feel them again through your more experienced eyes

Which ones you will see? Only you can know, but only look, never go down closer, keep your distance.

Tick tock

When the time is right you can go back forward

Fly along your line of time... all the way back through your life.

Until you get to now.

There you are, still in the same place.

"Hi"

You wave at yourself.

Let's go forward now

Remember it's the way that feels right for you and your future, off you go, float along forward.

How far you will go only you know, but when you are there it feels right, so you stop and look down.

That's you, you can see and you choose to see the you, you want to be, the you, you know is the best version of you, the real you the authentic you. You like this you. Go on, take a look.

You look good and you look happy, you are doing something you love doing and you look confident doing it.

Dressed in the clothes you like, that feel right they make you feel wonderful. You feel unique and you feel seen. Look at yourself, see yourself bright and sharp.

Let's go down this time.

You get closer and start to hear the sounds and feel the feelings you are feeling, we can climb inside your future you and really get a feel for you.

Breathe in the feelings of confidence and happiness that are surrounding this future version of yourself. This is the future you, this is how you are going to be, how you can be.

Tick tock

How are you standing? Lift your head, your chest your shoulders. Feel your peace, feel that this is how YOU are!

Balanced.

Take in a last deep breath of how this feels to be you and...

When it feels right, you float back up to your line of time, taking all the hope and joy and the possibility that you feel with you. It feels good.

In your own time, because again it's yours, you float back towards now and this time you come back down into to yourself now.

Tick tock, open your eyes.

Don't you feel great right now? After all, there's no time like the present!

Chapter Five

Who am I?

Letting go and being free

I am me... but who is me?

Am I lover, brother, sister, mother?

Am I lazy, crazy, like no other?

I am painter, sculptor, judge and jury

I am boss

I am worker

Am I who they say I am?

Why do I need to know so badly, why do I feel so lost?

I'm holding on as tight as I can

"I can help"

says a little voice from afar

"Who is that?"

There's no answer and I can't see who it is but I want to find myself, so say

"OK, how?"

The voice says

"You need to let yourself feel free to follow me and see where you might be"

I feel scared, I feel nervous but I want to know.

I say

"How do I do that?"

"You trust me"

says the voice

"I don't know you"

I say

"What DO you know?"

asks the voice

"I know I want to trust you. You seem nice"

"Then let's do what we need to do to find you"

the voice says.

"Close your eyes and imagine you are at the bottom of a ladder."

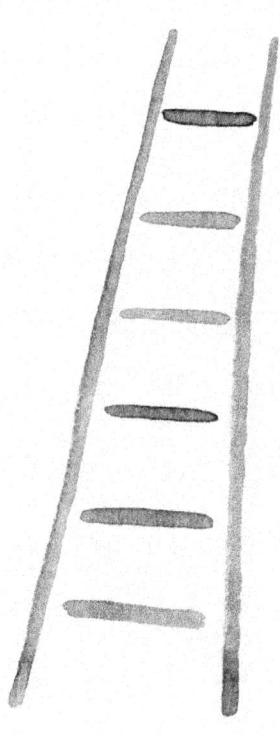

I say

"I don't like heights"

The voice laughs, but not in a mean way.

It softly says

"Oh silly, you do realise this is your ladder, so it can go whatever direction you want, up, down sideways, now just step onto the first rung and tell me where you are when you are feeling lost?"

"OK"

I say.

Because I do want to know who I am, and I do feel lost.

So I take a deep breath and I shut my eyes.

I step on the first rung and the voice asks gently,

"Where are you?"

I look and see myself at work. I'm at my desk and I feel everyone around me but they don't see me. I feel unhappy here, underwhelmed, overwhelmed. I don't know who I am here.

I don't know what I want.

I just know I don't like me here.

"OK"

says the voice

"Let's step onto the next rung. Tell me what are you doing?"

I step onto the next rung. I try to feel what I am doing. I'm not really doing anything. I'm bored, I hear other people doing, I'm surfing, I'm moaning, I'm blaming, I'm stuck.

"I'm not doing a good job."

The voice says

"Keep going."

So I step onto another rung.

"Now tell me what do you know there, what can you do?"

"I am looking, I am thinking, I am feeling.

I think I can do more, I can feel more, I can be more, I really want more.

Why aren't I doing more?"

I step onto the next rung.

I am thinking. "Why don't I believe I can?"

The voice asks

"What do you value?"

"I value respect, I value my family, I value my livelihood, I value life"

The voice says.

"And what DO you believe"

"I do believe I can do better, I really do"

"Next rung"

says the voice

"So where do you fit in?"

"Do I have to? I don't want to fit, I want to flip, I want to shout, I want to make a stir. I want to be different, to matter, to be heard."

I step up again, this rung is different.

I'm somewhere else, somewhere bigger. I'm somewhere safe

"Where am I?"

I ask

"You tell me"

says the voice.

"It's beautiful here, everything is so comfortable and calm"

It's a place beyond me.

I feel free, I look around and feel the light and warmth.

I drink it in, I let go.

I let it all go.

I stop trying so hard and just let go.

It feels amazing. I love it and I love me in it.

Why have I been trying so hard, it's exhausting. It feels so wonderful to stop.

I breathe, I smile, I feel at peace, time just stops.

Time goes by and I feel myself, I feel I know what it is to be me.

Now the voice says

"I want you to step back to the last rung"

"Why?"

I ask

"I want to stay here I'm so free here, it feels so right"

"But you are here"

the voice says

"Now see how that works on the ladder?"

"OK but I'm not sure. I really like me in this place"

"OK"

says the voice

"Where do you fit now?"

"I don't need to fit," I say, "I just am."

The voice continues

"What do you value and believe?"

"I value knowing that things are not always how I think they are, and I believe I'm at the top of a ladder"

"What are you doing now?"

"I'm scared but I'm staying"

"And where are you now?"

"I'm up, I'm down, I'm in the middle

I'm everywhere and nowhere

I realise I am wherever I want to be brave enough to be"

"So who are you then?"

says the voice

"Oh, finally"

I say

I take a long deep breath out and smile

"That's easy"

I say

I am You!

The End
but also the beginning...

Who we are

We are EqUa Coaching a transformative life and performance coaching company that works from the inside out.

We have used these tools, skills and methods to create our own unique approach - The EqUa Approach® and are dedicated to giving you the help you need to get yourself back into balance.

Over the years we have enabled clients to overcome anxiety, crippling fears, insomnia, to de-stress, to increase their performance and to battle their phobias.

Our clients have included television presenters, actors, comedians and business executives.

We love working with people from all walks of life and we find there is a common humanity when it comes to living our lives; from a stay at home parent to a CEO we are all in search of balance and happiness.

Looking forward to helping you take that first step.

Jo & Liz

EqUa Coaching

For more details visit our website:
www.equacoaching.com or our Facebook page.

For details of the audio version go to this page:
www.equacoaching.com/whoamiaudio

What is the EqUa Approach

The EqUa Approach is about finding balance in all aspects of your life with equilibrium, equality and equanimity. The EqUa Approach is a way to help you
get yourself into balance.

Balance of Mind
Balance of Body
Balance of life

When you have an even mind, you give yourself the best opportunity to live the life you want.

By using the techniques and teachings of this approach to help you calm your mind, raise your self-belief and become aware of you and your possibilities, you can gain control back and give yourself the freedom to do whatever you want.

> **"** With Equanimity, you can deal with situations with **calm and reason** while keeping your **inner happiness. "**
> The Dalai Lama

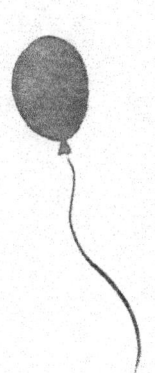

www.ingramcontent.com/pod-product-compliance
Lightning Source LLC
Chambersburg PA
CBHW031200020426
42333CB00013B/760